Leaves

Leaves

tanka anthology of Nature

collected and edited
by Amelia Fielden
assisted by Liz Lanigan

Leaves: tanka anthology of Nature
ISBN 978 1 76109 398 2
Copyright © poems individual authors 2022
Copyright © this collection Amelia Fielden 2022
Cover image: Neva Kastelic

First published 2022 by
GINNINDERRA PRESS
PO Box 3461 Port Adelaide 5015
www.ginninderrapress.com.au

Contributors

Ailsa Brown	9
Anne Benjamin	10
Barbara Curnow	11
Carmel Summers	12
Carole Harrison	13
Catherine McGrath	14
Gerry Jacobson	15
Glenys Ferguson	16
Hazel Hall	17
Jan Foster	18
Janne Graham	19
Jenny Stewart	20
Judy Young	21
Julia Emert	22
Kate King	23
Keitha Keyes	24
Liz Lanigan	25
Lois Holland	26
Margi Abraham	27
Marilyn Humbert	28
Meryl Turner	29
Michael Thorley	30
Michelle Brock	31
Mira Walker	32
Neal Whitman	33
Neva Kastelic	34

Owen Bullock	35
Paul Williamson	36
Peter Frankis	37
Rachel Colombo	38
Saeko Ogi	39
Samantha Sirimanne Hyde	40
Sue Donnelly	41
Tony Williams	42
Amelia Fielden	43

Preface: on leaves

The tanka form, in which these short lyrics on nature were composed, is that of traditional Japanese poetry. In classical Japanese, the expression meaning 'leaves', *kotonoha*, is a homonym for 'words'. Both are also written identically, in Kanji characters which join 'say' with 'leaf/leaves'. *Kotonoha* can also refer to *waka*, the pre-modern designation for tanka poems.

The first Japanese anthology of exclusively *waka* (tanka) poetry, is the *Kokin Wakashu, A Collection of Japanese Poetry, Old and New*, compiled in the tenth century. Its preface is considered to be one of the early masterpieces of Japanese prose, and the start of Japanese poetry criticism. Written by poet Ki no Tsurayuki (872–945), principal compiler and editor of the anthology, the preface begins, 'Japanese poetry has the human heart as seed and myriads of words as leaves.' He goes on to describe how poetry inspires emotions, comparing it to the sights, sounds, and feelings associated with nature.

rocky shoreline
emerges with daybreak,
its story
revealed in folds
of Ordovician time

~ ~ ~ ~

moonset at sunrise
autumn swim beneath pale sky
striped by contrails…
above and below
travellers through time

Ailsa Brown

with the rain
the silent shallows
swelling
finding their song
at last, among rocks

~ ~ ~

fluffy pink stamens
of a eucalypt blossom
on the pavement –
small unpretentious things
sometimes make a difference

Anne Benjamin

the white bobtail
of a rabbit hopping
on the hill…
so fluffy, so cute
this feral menace

~ ~ ~ ~

a distant crow
and one much closer
exchange calls –
it's time to talk
to my younger self

Barbara Curnow

the doldrums
for months on end…
in bare-boned trees
those noisy currawongs
might have some answers

~ ~ ~ ~

lower leaves turning
upper leaves vibrant green
a small crab apple
pauses, mid-season
my world holds its breath

Carmel Summers

so many
wombat homes flooded
by heavy rains…
the depths of hope
rebuilding for a third time

~ ~ ~ ~

a sand dollar
now slightly broken
on a long journey
I learn to celebrate
life's perfect imperfections

Carole Harrison

raging rivers
rip apart their banks
again climate
displays its mastery
of 'show not tell'

~~~~

in the bush
a brush turkey
this morning
and every morning
for 30 million years

Catherine McGrath

hunted
haunted, endangered
anteater
with the longest tongue
in the wet market of Wuhan

~~~~

a sack
full of autumn leaves
on my back
the weight of twenty million
covid casualties

Gerry Jacobson

day in day out
the old man and his wife
inseparable
two oystercatchers
dig for pipis together

~ ~ ~ ~

fingering
an aged flannel flower
…how soft
impressed in my old diary
those nights of love too

Glenys Ferguson

warbling a solo
on my recorder
I hear
like a ritornello
the magpies' answer

~ ~ ~ ~

postlude
to an amethyst sunset,
tonight the breeze
sings violets
in A flat major

Hazel Hall

it's been a day
of problems crowding in
…ducklings
tumble into the pond
paddling fast to stay afloat

~ ~ ~ ~

in the midst
of devastating floods
this small victory
a species rescued
…southern corroboree frog

Jan Foster

an echidna
ambles along the road…
I brake hard
here, a little life saved
elsewhere so much death

~ ~ ~ ~

sunflowers smile
across the Tuscan fields –
in Ukraine, they're
slashed by a shot-down plane,
destroyed by invaders

Janne Graham

cut a little
says a wispy native shrub,
but not too much…
make a decision
you with the rusty shears

~ ~ ~ ~

crazy cocky
lands on too-thin wire…
down he goes
then up, then down,
gymnast or battler

Jenny Stewart

currawong
beady yellow-eyed pirate
poised on the gutter
ready to raid my olive trees…
hose in hand, I meet his gaze

~ ~ ~ ~

a full moon
spills milk across dark water…
on the veranda
we watch in silence,
sipping our red wine

Judy Young

leaf spider
long lanky legs dangling,
winter's coming in
my clothes are outgrown too
let's spin ourselves some stockings

~ ~ ~ ~

in the blender
you just escaped your fate
small green crawler
you might be basil pesto –
what kind eye watches over me

Julia Emert

Wollemi pine
hidden for millennia
gorge deep
my love for him
rediscovered decades on

~ ~ ~ ~

knobbly seed pods
pounce from spiky bushes –
we still recoil
from those gumnut tales
of Big Bad Banksia Men

Kate King

a good sign
water is nearby,
that flock
of budgerigars
in the desert sky

~ ~ ~ ~

spring rain…
the red earth
gives birth
to a bumper crop
of paddymelons

Keitha Keyes

it's the best
climbing tree in Canberra
this apple box
not logged…perhaps they left it
for sheep to shelter here

~~~~

what's this red
on fallen she-oak needles
in the stream
Australia's autumn colours
the blood shed on this land

Liz Lanigan

those stars
in the Milky Way
glitter icily,
concealing hot core gases –
are you furious with me

~ ~ ~ ~

sometimes
I just sit in reverie –
upside down
on golden grevilleas
mynahs swinging, snacking

Lois Holland

a sudden storm
flings leaves and bark
across the lawn
…order in my life
is always fleeting

~ ~ ~ ~

you tell me
everything is fine
after the storm
barriers of driftwood
marking the tideline

Margi Abraham

we walk
beside a dry creek
speckled
with mussel shell shards
…our harvest of dust

~ ~ ~ ~

tailor bird:
I watch a tiny seamstress
make her nest
stitching cobwebs
to the edge of a leaf

Marilyn Humbert

tiny elm seeds
in tightly wrapped packages
twirl to the ground
leaving the mothership
on an autumn flight plan

~ ~ ~ ~

this wild wind
on the last day of winter
a tarantella
flirtation with spring –
where are my dancing shoes

Meryl Turner

a warm wind
scatters rose petals
on my path –
too late for the bride
who passed long ago

~ ~ ~ ~

night and day
the wagtail and I
whistle together –
what wouldn't I give
to know what we're saying

Michael Thorley

her terrarium
an overgrown jungle
in a jar
insurgent house plants
resist another lockdown

~~~~

always a fan
of elegant architecture,
she stops
in her tracks and ducks
under the spiderweb

Michelle Brock

our tabby
bewildered, legs knotted
with snakebite –
long tongues of drought
slide into the garden

~~~~

rosellas
nibble the callistemon's
juicy shoots –
we huddle with poems
savouring snippets

Mira Walker

goose droppings
on the 16th green
make putting
for birdie impossible –
the rule book of no use

~ ~ ~

across the park
pine saplings in plastic tubes
prompt us
embrace the pace of Nature
most good things take time

Neal Whitman
(California; guest poet)

to the shops
past cranes building out the sky…
an apricot tree
in someone's cramped backyard
shudders, and I walk on gold

~ ~ ~ ~

late autumn
most of the look-at-me leaves
have fallen…
now we're left with nothing but
the bare bones of reality

Neva Kastelic

on our walk
by the Fallen-Over-Tree
we eat plums
look at kangaroos
looking at us

Owen Bullock

high on a branch
a pale kestrel perches
short-tailed
just out of the nest
staring into the future

~ ~ ~ ~

winter days
begin to lengthen,
wattle blooms
telling Ngunnawal people
First Spring has come

Paul Williamson

a royal spoonbill
sashays down the floodline
flings back his plumes
like Elvis at Vegas
man, he just owns this swamp

~~~~

enormous moon
rising over rooftops,
yellow hibiscus
spilling over your fence…
neighbours stop, stare open-mouthed

Peter Frankis

two rock doves
huddle on the powerline
sharing its warmth
an elderly couple
snuggle under a heater

~ ~ ~ ~

lone cherry tree
in the wintry Kyiv street
a bomb explodes,
days later buds burst
showering pink blossom

Rachel Colombo

neat gardeners
tidying dropped leaves,
ignorant
of the masked plovers'
peace beneath the shrubs

~ ~ ~

in the gardens
of this retirement village
bright tulips
from last winter's covid bulbs
are dancing Floriade

Saeko Ogi

autumn breeze…
within the pleached hedge
patches of blue,
tiny glimpses that cheer
our lockdown strolling

~ ~ ~ ~

embowered
among the rampant weeds
a Buddha's head
its limestone weathered
its features smoothed

Samantha Sirimanne Hyde

noisy koel
calling in moonlight…
listen
enjoy the moment
the blessing of sound

Sue Donnelly

arching the ocean
a rainbow loses focus –
how I wish
we could cloud-store good dreams
before they disappear

Tony Williams

in full thrum
cicadas emphasising
the summer days –
less is more, I tell
my tanka students

~ ~ ~ ~

a little skink
slithers across my path
into long grass –
keeping a low profile
with Omicron rampant

~ ~ ~ ~

seagulls flapping
in a fresh water pool
apparently
rinsing salt from their wings –
all the things I'm still learning

Amelia Fielden

www.ingramcontent.com/pod-product-compliance
Lightning Source LLC
Chambersburg PA
CBHW070340120526
44590CB00017B/2962